ANGER MANAGEMENT

Control & Manage Your Anger to Inspire a Healthier, Stress-Free Life

Table of Contents

Introduction

The human experience is characterized by a wide range of feelings and emotions that individuals go through in various situations. When you win a ball game or get that promotion you've worked for so long, you feel happiness. When a loved one passes away or when you say goodbye to a pet, you feel sadness. Excitement is felt when you are planning a special day such as a wedding or birthday bash, or when you are about to go on a dream vacation. Meanwhile, before a difficult examination or a contentious meeting, nervousness can set in.

What makes these feelings unique is how you, as the person feeling them, can manage, control, or deal with these normal emotions, regardless of what the circumstances surrounding you may be. Emotionally intelligent people are able to control their emotions and work them to their own benefit. These feelings are normal and often unavoidable, but your character and resolve will determine how you manage your reactions and steps when going through emotionally-charged situations.

Anger is another human emotion that many people struggle with. On any given day, you may feel varying levels of anger directed towards people, things, situations, and other external factors. But it is your reaction or your response to the highly volatile emotion of anger that can spell the difference between a potentially destructive situation, the termination of an important friendship or work relationship, or even the end of a romantic partnership.

It cannot be denied that, in so many instances, situations that can lead to anger can not be avoided. Even just a casual remark, an unfinished task, a careless decision made by someone, can lead you to become angry. It may not even have to be directed toward any one person necessarily. Anger can be triggered by a traffic jam, a delayed flight, or a missed train ride. But as you assess how you deal with potential anger triggers, are you reacting in a controlled, rational, and collected manner when faced with this emotion, or does anger take over how you think, act, and decide, leading to regrettable consequences?

Anger is associated with a lot of violent crime in our society. In the 2011 article "What Causes Someone to Act on Violent Impulses and Commit Murder?" on the *Scientific American*, University of California

Los Angeles professor Marco Iacoboni, who teaches psychiatry and biobehavioral sciences and also directs the university's Transcranial Magnetic Stimulation Laboratory, said about anger and violent predispositions, "Self-control is key to a well-functioning life, because our brain makes us easily susceptible to all sorts of influences. Watching a movie showing violent acts predisposes us to act violently. Even just listening to violent rhetoric makes us more inclined to be violent. Ironically, the same mirror neurons that make us empathic make us also very vulnerable to all sorts influences."

He adds, "This is why control mechanisms are so important. Indeed, after many years of studies on mirror neurons and their functioning we are shifting our lab research to the study of the control mechanisms in the brain for mirror neurons. If you think about it, there must be control mechanisms for mirror neurons. Mirror neurons are cells that fire when I grab a cup of coffee (to give you an example) as well as when I see you grabbing a cup of coffee. So, how come I don't imitate you all the time? The idea is that there are systems in the brain that help us by imitating only "internally"—they dampen the activity of mirror neurons when we simply watch, so that we can still have the sort of "inner imitation" that allows us to empathize with others, without any overt imitation."

Balance is important, as Iacoboni points out. "The key issue is the balance of power between these control mechanisms that we call top-down—because they are all like executives that control from the top down to the employees—and bottom-up mechanisms, in the opposite direction, like mirror neurons. Whereby perception—watching somebody making an action—influences decisions—making the same action ourselves."

Triggers are all around you, but what you can do to resolve them is to correctly and rationally manage what your response would be when faced with anger, and how to not lose control. Over the next few chapters, you will read more about the underlying characteristics of anger and understand the best ways to manage it.

Chapter One: Understanding Anger

Psychologist Charles Spielberger, Ph.D., a specialist in the study of anger in humans, defines anger as "an emotional state that varies in intensity from mild irritation to intense fury and rage". According to the *Encyclopedia of Psychology*, it is "an emotion characterized by antagonism toward someone or something you feel has deliberately done you wrong. Anger can be a good thing. It can give you a way to express negative feelings, for example, or motivate you to find solutions to problems. But excessive anger can cause problems. Increased blood pressure and other physical changes associated with anger make it difficult to think straight and harm your physical and mental health."

Part of our human instinct when experiencing anger is to react or to lash out aggressively. The American Psychological Association, in its definition of anger, says, "The instinctive, natural way to express anger is to respond aggressively. Anger is a natural, adaptive response to threats; it inspires powerful, often aggressive, feelings and behaviours, which allow us to fight and to defend ourselves when we are attacked. A certain amount of anger, therefore, is necessary to our survival."

While it can be attributed partly to the human survival instinct, it is also important to note that responding aggressively is not always the right reaction. "On the other hand, we can't physically lash out at every person or object that irritates or annoys us; laws, social norms, and common sense place limits on how far our anger can take us. People use a variety of both conscious and unconscious processes to deal with their angry feelings. The three main approaches are expressing, suppressing, and calming. Expressing your angry feelings in an assertive—non aggressive—manner is the healthiest way to express anger. To do this, you have to learn how to make clear what your needs are, and how to get them met, without hurting others. Being assertive doesn't mean being pushy or demanding; it means being respectful of yourself and others," according to the APA.

As previously mentioned briefly in the previous chapter, anger has been closely associated with violent crime, particularly anger that has been repressed, triggered, or left unmanaged for particularly long periods of time. Writing for *Slate.com*, Laura L. Hayes explains in the article "How to Stop Violence", Violence is not a product of mental illness. Nor is violence generally the action of ordinary, stable individuals who suddenly "break" and commit crimes of passion. Violent crimes are committed by violent people, those who do not have the skills to manage their anger. Most homicides are committed by people with a history of violence. Murderers are rarely ordinary, law-abiding citizens, and they are also rarely mentally ill. Violence is a product of compromised anger management skills.

The statistics reveal the link between unresolved anger and a tendency to commit violent crimes, as Hayes points out. "In a summary of studies on murder and prior records of violence, Don Kates and Gary Mauser found that 80 to 90 percent of murderers had prior police records, in contrast to 15 percent of American adults overall. In a study of domestic murderers, 46 percent of the perpetrators had a restraining order against them at some time. Family murders are preceded by prior domestic violence more than 90 percent of the time. Violent crimes are committed by people who lack the skills to modulate anger, express it constructively, and move beyond it."

When violent crimes make the headlines these days, too often mental illness is pointed out as a culprit or trigger. While mental health problems do play a role in some violent crimes, the facts suggest that they are actually in the minority. In her article, Hayes again refers to the statistics. "Violent crimes committed by people with severe mental illnesses get a lot of attention, but such attacks are relatively rare. Paolo del Vecchio of the federal Substance Abuse and Mental Health Services Administration has said, "Violence by those with mental illness is so small that even if you could somehow cure it all, 95 percent of violent crime would still exist." A 2009 study by Seena Fazel found a slightly higher rate of violent crime in schizophrenics—but it was almost entirely accounted for by alcohol and drug abuse. Likewise, the

MacArthur Violence Risk Assessment Study found that mentally ill people who did not have a substance abuse problem were no more violent than other people in their neighbourhoods."

The sad fact is that anger management is not being focused on as much as it should be in determining the root cause of many crimes perpetuated in our society today. "With no clear explanation of the causes of violent crime from the mental health field, and with significant encouragement from the gun lobby, the public has begun to seize on the wrong explanation for tragic, violent events. They focus not on the IED-diagnosed patients but on those with other diagnoses, schizophrenia in particular, ignoring the fact that what the perpetrators have in common in every single one of these cases is a loss of control of their anger," the article explains.

Hayes adds, "The attribution of violent crime to people diagnosed with mental illness is increasing stigmatization of the mentally ill while virtually no effort is being made to address the much broader cultural problem of anger management. This broader problem encompasses not just mass murders but violence toward children and spouses, rape, road rage, assault, and violent robberies. We are a culture awash in anger."

Now, it of course does not necessarily mean that if you are constantly experiencing feelings of anger in varying levels, then you are likely to commit murder, homicide, or other violent crimes. But in so many instances, aside from many possible triggers in the environment, background, or mental and emotional circumstances surrounding a person's reaction to feelings of anger, the underlying cause would also be the lack of a clear understanding and appreciation of the magnitude of anger management.

How should you respond accordingly? An understanding of anger and how it can affect your thinking, your reasoning, and your actions would be crucial to managing this emotion in a responsible way. You will need an honest assessment of what causes you to be angry, and how to either prepare yourself to respond without losing your cool, avoiding the conflict altogether, or how to mitigate any effects that may arise as the feelings of anger emerge.

Ideally, a proper understanding of anger management should begin early on in life. Hayes writes in her article for *Slate.com,* "The violence that is a part of anger disorders is fuelled by chronic repressed rage that has found no socially acceptable outlet. It is fostered by families in which adults behave in violent, intimidating ways or in which anger is tightly repressed. In either situation there is no appropriate model for the safe or constructive expression of anger ... One of the allegations that have recently been made is that the mental health community is failing society in dealing with violent crime. I would agree with this assessment. We have failed to provide an appropriate diagnosis for out-of-control anger or a framework to assist people in understanding the senseless violence around them, and worse, we have done nothing to prevent it."

She asserts, "The truth is, anger management skills are simple techniques that can and should be taught to children and adolescents. We should not wait to teach these skills until verbally or physically violent behaviour has become habitual and, often, life-threatening."

The good news is that there are plenty of resources you can turn to if you are interested in anger management and how to best deal with this in your daily life. There are professionals who can offer their valuable expertise and advice to you, and techniques that are constantly being studied and perfected in order to help individuals struggling with controlling their feelings of anger. You just have to be willing to really look within, get to the root of the problem, and be open to ideas that would lead to healthy change.

Chapter Two: The Different Types of Anger

It may be easy to just dismiss or generalize anger as one type of emotion, but if we look at it closely there are actually different types or profiles of anger that humans experience. Many of these types of anger profiles are related to each other, and you may move from one type of anger to another within a period of time, sometimes longer or shorter, depending on the circumstances around you or what has triggered your emotional outburst. Let us take a look at the common anger types and how you can identify them.

Passive anger. Passive anger may also be referred to as resistant anger, and this is characterized by silence or repression. This type of anger is either unacknowledged or attempted to be kept inside, but may manifest itself in snide comments or remarks, or passive aggressive statements made either directly to a person involved or others around you. If you have ever been annoyed or irritated at a person or a situation, but have kept it inside or have just mentioned a comment to another person, this could be a sign of passive anger.

Passive or resistant anger can be quite hard to manage, and it has also been shown to have negative effects on a person's health especially if left unchecked for a long period of time. In an interview with *EverydayHealth.com,* New York-based psychologist Peter Sacco, Ph.D. mentions, "When you keep the feelings all bottled up, your body is tense all the time. Your immune system weakens, and you're at higher risk for heart disease, cancer, osteoarthritis, even temporomandibular joint dysfunction and skin conditions. It's not uncommon for this type of person to one day just snap."

Passive anger, or passive aggressive behaviour, could be used by many people because in general, society frowns upon obvious outbursts of anger or confrontation. Writing for *Psychology Today,* Signe Whitson L.S.W. comments, "Anger is a normal, natural human emotion. It is, in fact, one of the most basic of all human experiences. Yet from a very young age, many of us are bombarded with the message that anger is bad. During a period in our emotional development when we are highly susceptible to social pressure from parents, caregivers, and teachers, we learn that to be "good" we must squash honest self-expression and hide angry feelings ... When people learn that they cannot express anger openly, honestly, and directly within relationships, the emotion doesn't just go away. Rather, many of us learn to express it in alternative, covert, socially acceptable ways, often through passive aggressive behaviours."

Whitson also mentions that in a lot of situations, passive-aggressive behaviour could be seem like the easier way out. "In this day and age of common core, standardized tests, and Race to the Top, social skills instruction is often edged out of a young person's formal education. Yet study after study shows that specific instruction in such "soft" skills as assertiveness, emotion management, and relationship building are as essential to a young person's development as any "hard core" math and reading skills ... Not everyone who uses passive aggressive behaviour is a passive aggressive person. For example, a husband who typically communicates directly and honestly with his wife may not have the wherewithal on a particular weekend day to say "no" to her request to fix a leaky faucet, so he promises to do it while making endless excuses to put off the task. The man is not passive aggressive across the board, but on this day when relaxing and avoiding a fight with his wife are his top priorities, he chooses passive aggression as a convenient behaviour of choice."

Volatile anger. This type of anger is also closely related to intermittent explosive disorder. Volatile anger is characterized by sudden outbursts of anger that are exaggerated or larger in proportion to the size of the circumstance or trigger surrounding it. Chris Aiken, M.D. director of the Mood Treatment Center and a clinical psychiatry instructor at Wake Forest University School of Medicine in North Carolina explains, "In intermittent explosive disorder, people shift into sudden and extreme bouts of anger that are out of character for them, almost like a seizure."

EverydayHealth.com postulates that this anger profile is seen more in males or those with certain conditions related to substance abuse. "Volatile anger is slightly more common in males and those with substance abuse problems. This type of anger puts people at risk for self-harm, damage to property, violence against others, and trouble with interpersonal relationships. It's important to seek professional help for patterns of this type of anger, and to use caution if someone around you is prone to it."

Volatile anger often requires professional treatment, especially if intermittent explosive disorder is diagnosed. The Mayo Clinic describes intermittent explosive disorder as such: "Explosive eruptions occur suddenly, with little or no warning, and usually last less than 30 minutes. These episodes may occur frequently or be separated by weeks or months of nonaggression. Less severe verbal outbursts may occur in between episodes of physical aggression. You may be irritable, impulsive, aggressive or chronically angry most of the time. Aggressive episodes may be preceded or accompanied by rage, irritability, increased energy, racing thoughts, tingling, tremors, palpitations, chest tightness."

Chronic anger. Anger that is left unchecked or unresolved over a long period of time can be classified as chronic anger. When anger becomes a habit for the person, it becomes part of their daily life and can lead to many health problems, particularly a weaker immune system. Peter Sacco, Ph.D. describes a chronically angry person: "This is a person who gets into the habit of anger. He or she wakes up pissed off, and moves angrily from one thing to the next, setting the day up in their mind as 'Here we go again.' He or she is always looking for something to get angry about. Left untreated, this is the type of person who ends up in trouble with the law or alienates him or herself from family and friends."

Mike Brundant, who writes "NLP Discoveries" in the *PsychCentral.com* site, says, "Chronic anger is so damaging to your body that it may out rank smoking, obesity and a high-fat diet as a risk factor for chronic disease and early death. Worse, no one seems to know what to do with it. You shouldn't suppress anger, say some, as that only enhances the physical damage. You shouldn't vent it either, say others, as that only enhances the physical damage! Anger is maddening."

Chronic anger has been linked to heart diseases, high blood pressure, migraines and chronic headaches, skin disorders, digestive problems, fatigue, chronic pain, and alcohol or substance abuse, among other effects.

Vengeful anger. Vengeful anger is characterized by a near-obsession or extreme fascination with a person whom you feel has done you wrong, often with thoughts of getting even. Dr. Chris Aiken, M.D. cautions that this type of anger can drain you mentally, emotionally, and even physically, causing stress and a host of health problems. "Studies find that when someone wrongs you and you are given the opportunity to take revenge, the dopamine or reward center in the brain gets activated in a similar manner to addictions. In other words, revenge is sweet and addictive, which explains the tendency for angry people to ruminate over vengeful themes that get more and more intense as the thinking progresses."

Finding something else to occupy yourself with is one step to defeating vengeful anger. "A good approach for this type of anger is to find activities that get you out if your head, such as volunteering, which shifts your brain from anger at others toward helping others," says Dr. Aiken.

The *American Psychological Association* points out that feelings of revenge have been around for as long as humans have had to deal with each other relationally. Historically, there are two schools of thought on revenge. The Bible, in Exodus 21:23, instructs us to "give life for life, eye for eye, tooth for tooth, hand for hand, foot for foot" to punish an offender. But more than 2,000 years later, Martin Luther King Jr., responded, "The old law of 'an eye for an eye' leaves everybody blind."

Michael Price writes for the *APA*, "Who's right? As psychologists explore the mental machinery behind revenge, it turns out both can be, depending on who and where you are. If you're a power-seeker, revenge can serve to remind others you're not to be trifled with. If you live in a society where the rule of law is weak, revenge provides a way to keep order. But revenge comes at a price. Instead of helping you move on with your life, it can leave you dwelling on the situation and remaining unhappy, psychologists' research finds. Considering revenge is a very human response to feeling slighted, humans are atrocious at predicting its effects."

Petrified anger. Also referred to as hardened anger, this type of anger happens when you become bitter towards a person or situation and find it hard to forgive, forget, and move on. Dr. Peter Sacco answers about petrified anger, "This is when someone hangs on to a sense of hatred and bitterness. You're waiting for an apology, but the person who did it maybe doesn't care or doesn't even know that you're mad ... You've got to realize that the anger isn't getting you anywhere. Even if you're no longer in touch with the person, you can choose to forgive them once and for all, and by doing so you'll forgive yourself."

The longer you are holding on to the hurt, frustration, or disappointment caused by someone else, the more bitter you become and the harder those feelings of anger in your heart become. Eventually, you can get used to harbouring these feelings of resentment and begin to think of these emotions as normal in your daily life.

Incidental anger. Sometimes, anger is characterized by a sudden outburst that immediately gets resolved or leads to proper action once it is dealt with. Incidental anger can arise from an unexpected event or unforeseen circumstance, and it can be expressed in a proper way to the right person involved, leading to immediate rectification.

Cynthia Pavlock of The Center for Anger Resolution in Houston, Texas states, "Anger is not a bad or terrible emotion; it helps us to sense that something is wrong. It's great to have an anger-provoking incident, appropriately express it and then move on."

Empathic or sympathetic anger. This type of anger can also be a healthy emotion if it leads to proper change or action. Empathic anger refers to anger on behalf of someone else, especially a person who was wronged or unjustly treated. Empathic anger can lead you to take action or start a worthy cause on behalf of someone, primarily because of the righteous indignation you felt for another person or cause.

For instance, if a neighbour in your community was unjustly treated, you may become very angry on their behalf and start a petition calling on your neighbourhood to support the person or family and help get justice, or demand that proper action be applied. Dr. Chris Aiken says, "Mental health usually improves when we focus on others rather than ourselves, despite the frequent popular advice to schedule self-time and self-care. For example, people report greater happiness when they do volunteer work directly face-to-face helping others, versus doing the same work with pay."

Chapter Three: Why Am I Always Angry?

Anger, as already mentioned, is part of our wide range of human emotions. It is perfectly normal to feel anger at times, whether it is anger relating to a person, a group, a situation, or a circumstance. But what is not normal, and what can be destructive to your mental, emotional, and physical well-being, is anger that is constant, unnecessary, or left unresolved. When anger becomes a habit or a part of a never-ending cycle, it begins to manifest negative results in your overall well-being, hindering you from becoming your best self.

However, if you can identify at least some of the reasons why you are experiencing anger, or get to the root causes of the emotion, perhaps there are steps you can take to minimize or avoid the conflict altogether. While there are situations that are completely unexpected, there may also be triggers or causes that can be properly identified and managed so you can lessen the instances in which you experience anger.

Frustration. Sometimes, anger stems from frustration when you are trying to fix a problem and failing at it, or encountering difficulty in learning a new thing. Frustration can happen when you are setting up a new home appliance and finding the user manual far too complicated. It can also be a frustration directed at co-workers who are not fulfilling their responsibilities, or family members who are not keeping their promises.

Frustration can lead to anger especially if you have set expectations and realize that those expectations are not being fulfilled. When you feel irritated and anger sets in, it helps to pause for a moment, take a step back, and think to yourself, "What else can I do to achieve the result that I am looking for?" Sometimes, anger can cause you to think irrationally and respond in ways that do not help the situation, but actually compound the problem, leading to more frustration on your part.

Instead of lashing out, try to think of an alternative action or solution. When you are angry or frustrated, you may feel a sudden urge to take action, and this energy can be directed not towards a person, but on finding a solution for the issue instead. This way, you can harness the emotion of anger and begin to use it towards something that would be beneficial rather than destructive.

It also helps to minimize frustration when you set reasonable expectations to start with. Writing for *Psychology Today*, Jennice Vilhauer, Ph. D. states, "The majority of anger and frustration we experience in life occurs when we encounter someone who is not playing by our rules. We tend to believe that our rules are right and that the other person should do it our way. At the basis of all conflict is the idea that one person believes another person should change. Stating that your rules are right, forces someone else's rules to be wrong. Personal rulebooks however, aren't right or wrong, they simply reflect the unique perspective and preferences of every individual. Many people find this a challenging notion to accept, but we live in a world of great diversity and there are no universal concepts that apply to every religion, race, or culture."

Fear or powerlessness. Anger is occasionally a by-product of fear. When changes are introduced and you do not know exactly how you will adjust to them, or when it appears you are about to embark on something where you are not totally in control, your fear may lead you to become angry at the situation or annoyed at the people who are implementing or causing changes. Fear of losing, being late, looking like you do not know what you are doing, or making a big mistake can all lead you to become agitated and angry.

Anger can also come from a feeling of powerlessness in a situation. When things are not going as planned and you just do not have total control over the circumstances, your reaction may be to become angry. Perhaps you have felt this anger if you have ever planned a big outdoor party with lots of guests, only to encounter inclement weather which could ruin the plans altogether. You realize you are powerless to control the weather, and compounded with the fear of failing miserably as the party host, you begin to get angry and annoyed at everyone.

If you are experiencing fear, try to identify exactly what it is that is causing you to be afraid. Is it the uncertainty of the future? Is it the risks involved in the new venture or direction? Whatever may be causing the anxiety, an angry response will not benefit the situation and will likely not even cause any changes to the reality of the circumstances. The same thing goes for powerlessness. Instead of being angry at other people who may not have any control over the situation as well, an alternative solution should be sought out in order to regain some control over the process.

Past hurt or pain. Humans experience pain and heartaches in various forms throughout life, and many times these can also be triggers for anger at current situations or people. Writing for *Psychology Today,* Dr. Leon F. Seltzer, Ph.D. explains, "In Steven Stosny's excellent book Treating Attachment Abuse (1995), which delineates a comprehensive model for therapeutically dealing with both physical and emotional violence in close relationships, the author offers a chemical explanation of how anger—in the moment at least—can act as a sort of "psychological salve." One of the hormones the brain secretes during anger arousal is norepinephrine, experienced by the organism as an analgesic. In effect, whether individuals are confronted with physical or psychological pain (or the threat of such pain), the internal activation of the anger response will precipitate the release of a chemical expressly designed to numb it."

He writes further, "As Stosny describes it, symptomatic anger covers up the pain of our "core hurts." These key distressful emotions include feeling ignored, unimportant, accused, guilty, untrustworthy, devalued, rejected, powerless, unlovable—or even unfit for human contact. It is, therefore, only reasonable that if the self-elicitation of anger can successfully fend off such hurtful or unbearable feelings, one might eventually become dependent on the emotion to the point of addiction. The psychological concept of self-soothing is unquestionably relevant here. For we all need to find ways of comforting or reassuring ourselves when our self-esteem is endangered—whether through criticism, dismissal, or any other outside stimuli that feels invalidating and so revives old self-doubts. If we're healthy psychologically, then we have the internal resources to self-validate: to admit to ourselves possible inadequacies without experiencing intolerable guilt or shame. But if, deep down, we still feel bad about who we are, our deficient sense of self simply won't be able to withstand such external threats."

If you are experiencing chronic anger because of something that has happened in the past, it would help to seek counselling or advice from a professional who can assist you in sorting it out and allowing you to recover from the pain of yesterday to be able to become a better person today. You may think that the anger helps you cope, but in reality it is doing a lot more damage to you physically and emotionally. Beth Darnall, Ph.D. says, "Among people with chronic pain, feelings of injustice and anger are associated with worse medical outcomes and greater pain. There may be many different reasons why these emotions have a negative impact on health. Anger causes increased tension in the body and this in turn increases pain. Anger is associated with increased inflammation in the body and this can worsen pain and overall health. Feelings of anger and injustice can keep you focused on what's wrong and who is to blame for it. Remind yourself that focusing on it gives it more energy."

Fatigue or exhaustion. Many people do not realize it, but constant fatigue or exhaustion, both physically and mentally, can also be a trigger for feelings of anger. When you are always overwhelmed or tired and not getting enough rest or time to refresh, you may become easily irritable and angry at either people or situations. Sherrie Bourg Carter Psy.D. explains, "Because burnout victims often feel like a failure and experience a lot of guilt, it's not uncommon for these feelings to turn into anger and resentment as the stress continues and you feel as if you have no control over it. At first, the anger may take the form of interpersonal tension with colleagues, family, or friends. As burnout becomes more severe, the anger may intensify and result in angry outbursts and serious arguments at home and in the workplace. You may have thoughts of violence toward co-workers or family, and at its most extreme, this may cross the line into actual violence."

The body, mind, and spirit need time to recover from the daily rigors of life. This means you should be getting the recommended number of hours of sleep each night, and also have time to take a break from your responsibilities and allow yourself to relax and renew from time to time. If you are not getting enough rest and recovery, you become so physically and mentally fatigued that actions and thoughts become too taxing, and anger may be the easiest or most convenient reaction to turn to.

If you have identified fatigue or over-exhaustion as reasons for your chronic anger, take some time to allow yourself to get much-needed rest and refreshment. A hobby or leisurely activity that takes your mind away from the daily hustle and bustle of life will do wonders for your well-being. Disconnecting from work, business, or other responsibilities even for just a few days and just immersing in total relaxation will allow you to find your inner peace, reflect, reconnect with your spirit, rekindle your relationship with your loved ones, and become more energized and able to think and respond rationally rather than in anger. You will be surprised in how effective this simple idea can be.

Jealousy or envy. Do you get angry or irritated when others get a promotion or award which you feel should have been yours or they do not really deserve? Are you constantly feeling mad when you are on social media and others are posting about vacations or new possessions? If so, feelings of jealousy or envy may be what is triggering your chronic anger, and this can become a very unhealthy habit.

Jealousy is not just related to possessions or material success. It may also be a feeling that you get when someone you love becomes attached to another person and you feel left out. Jealousy and envy can also arise from feelings of competition, or somehow getting it in your head that you are out there to outdo everyone else.

Perhaps the most common relationship where jealousy is discussed is between spouses. Robert L. Leahy, Ph.D., writing for *Psychology Today,* notes, "Jealousy is angry agitated worry. When we are jealous we worry that our partner might find someone else more appealing and we fear that he or she will reject us. Since we feel threatened that our partner might find someone more attractive, we may activate jealousy as a way to cope with this threat. We may believe that our jealousy may keep us from being surprised, help us defend our rights, and force our partner to give up interests elsewhere. Similar to worry, jealousy may be a "strategy" that we use so that we can figure out what is going wrong or learn what our partner "really feels." We may also think that our jealousy can motivate us to give up on the relationship—so that we don't get hurt any more. If you are feeling jealous, it's important to ask yourself what you hope to gain by your jealousy. We view jealousy as a coping strategy."

Leahy points out that how you act or respond to jealousy and feelings of anger spells the difference. "Just as there is a difference between feeling angry and acting in a hostile way, there is a difference between feeling jealous and acting on your jealousy. It's important to realize that your relationship is more likely to be jeopardized by your jealous behaviour—such as continual accusations, reassurance-seeking, pouting, and acting-out. Stop and say to yourself, 'I know that I am feeling jealous, but I don't have to act on it'."

Instead of lashing out, collect yourself and do not allow the emotion to take over. "Notice that your feeling of anger and anxiety may increase while you stand back and observe these experiences. Accept that you can have an emotion—and allow it to be. You don't have to "get rid of the feeling." We have found that mindfully standing back and observing that a feeling is there can often lead to the feeling weakening on its own," Dr. Leahy suggests.

Hyperthyroidism. Aside from situational triggers, anger may also be triggered or compounded by medical conditions, such as an overactive thyroid. This condition happens when the thyroid gland produces an excessive amount of the thyroid hormone. Hyperthyroidism has been linked to various manifestations such as metabolism problems, difficulty in concentration or focus, nervousness, anxiety, and restlessness. If you have been diagnosed with an overactive thyroid, it may be wise to talk to your physician about any chronic anger issues you are also experiencing and how this can be mitigated.

Dr. Neil Gittoes, an endocrinologist at the University Hospitals Birmingham and BMI The Priory Hospital, told the Daily Mail in an interview, "This hormone affects everything to do with the body's metabolism, including heart rate and body temperature. Circulating hormones affect every tissue, including the brain. Other symptoms may include weight loss, tremors and sweats. This is easy to rectify with medication such as Carbimazole, which stops the gland producing excess hormones."

High or low cholesterol. You are certainly aware how high cholesterol is often a harbinger of many other serious and life-threatening diseases and conditions. Many people with high cholesterol take medications to lower their cholesterol levels and reduce the risk of heart disease, but when cholesterol is too low, one unintended effect may be temper problems or anger.

According to Steve Bazire, an honorary professor at the University of East Anglia School of Pharmacy, "One theory is that low cholesterol levels also lower levels of serotonin (the happiness hormone) in the brain, making the response to anger harder to control. The risk of depression is highest with low and high levels of cholesterol, so being in the low to middle range seems the safest place to be. The best way to avoid this side-effect is to bring levels down slowly."

Diabetes. Diabetes is a disease that affects millions of people of all ages worldwide. It has also been linked to mood swings and outbursts of anger, aggression, and rage. An article in the *Daily Mail* entitled "The illnesses and medicines that could be to blame for your bad moods", this description is given: "Low blood sugar levels can cause sudden bursts of anger. Hypoglycaemia, caused by lower than normal blood glucose levels, can happen in type 1 and type 2 diabetes. Low sugar levels affect all body tissue, including the brain, and can lead to an imbalance of chemicals, including serotonin. Within minutes this can lead to aggression, anger, confusion, restlessness and panic attacks. Treatment involves drinking or eating something sugary as soon as possible and, fortunately, you should feel better within 20 minutes."

Depression. Depression is often associate with feelings of lethargy, sadness, or wanting to just lie down in bed all day or sulk in a corner, avoiding all contact with the outside word. Many times, however, depression can manifest itself into bouts of uncontrolled or unprovoked anger. Paul Blenkiron, a psychiatrist at the Bootham Park Hospital in York, says depression "It can also leave you feeling angry, agitated and irritable."

Dr. Helen Stokes-Lampard from the Royal College of General Practitioners asserts, "One extreme form, agitated depression, is thought to affect five per cent of people with depression. Symptoms can also include restlessness, insomnia and racing thoughts. Why one person is more likely to turn aggressive than another is often down to personality. Some people are simply more angry and aggressive in the first place and the medication or conditions enhance this."

Epilepsy. If you are suffering from epilepsy, you may also experience bouts of anger, aggression, or irritability after an epileptic seizure. Dr. Hannah Cock, a neurologist working at London's St. George's Hospital, explains, "Seizures themselves are caused by a sudden burst of electrical activity in the brain. This causes a temporary disruption in the normal message passing between brain cells. If the seizure is major, outbursts of anger, sometimes delusional, may occur afterwards."

At times, the effects of the epileptic seizure manifesting as irritability or anger may last for only a few minutes after the seizure, but for others the feelings may last for up to a few days after. In this case, the recommended treatment is anti-epileptic medication which would help not only with the seizures but also with the after-effects.

Sleeping pills. Medical experts have established a link between sleeping aids and being more irritable or prone to anger. In the Daily Mail article, a warning was raise regarding sleeping pills for curing insomnia which may be contributing to bouts of anger. "The group of drugs, known as benzodiazepines, also sometimes prescribed for anxiety, work by slowing down brain function. While affecting only one per cent of users, for those with an aggressive personality, this could make them even more prone to irrational outbursts. Ask your doctor to change to another type of sleeping tablet such as Zolpidem or Zaleplon."

Chapter Four: Anger Management Tips

As you become more aware of the triggers or causes of your anger, you can then better identify how to lessen the situations that cause you to become angry, or how you can manage this emotion so that you are in better control. Making small changes or adapting little reminders to your daily life can make a world of a difference in controlling your temper and making you more calm and collected even when confronted by people or situations that would normally cause you to lose control.

Here are some tips you can consider for better anger management:

Think first. When the stimuli or trigger shows up, it is very easy for emotions to flare up and immediately take control of your thoughts, actions, words, and reactions. Make it a habit to think first when confronted by anything or anyone that normally causes you to become irritable or frustrated. Stop yourself and pause for a few seconds before doing or saying anything. You do not have to immediately react to the circumstance, but all you need to do first is just pause.

Acknowledge and express your anger. Once you have had a moment to think, and have hopefully collected yourself, it is a good idea to express your anger in a calm, rational, and civilized way. Whether this is just acknowledging to yourself that you are angry, or expressing it to the person or people involved, expressing anger is better than sweeping it under the rug. When it is expressed, there is a better chance of finding the right solution for the conflict. But when anger is ignored or kept hidden, it can manifest itself in other ways that would be more detrimental.

The American Psychological Association (APA) says, "Anger can be suppressed, and then converted or redirected. This happens when you hold in your anger, stop thinking about it, and focus on something positive. The aim is to inhibit or suppress your anger and convert it into more constructive behaviour. The danger in this type of response is that if it isn't allowed outward expression, your anger can turn inward—on yourself. Anger turned inward may cause hypertension, high blood pressure, or depression."

The APA article continues to explain, "Unexpressed anger can create other problems. It can lead to pathological expressions of anger, such as passive-aggressive behaviour (getting back at people indirectly, without telling them why, rather than confronting them head-on) or a personality that seems perpetually cynical and hostile. People who are constantly putting others down, criticizing everything, and making cynical comments haven't learned how to constructively express their anger. Not surprisingly, they aren't likely to have many successful relationships."

Identify a solution. Acknowledge anger, and then figure out a way to resolve the situation. An article entitled "Anger Management: 10 Tips to Tame Your Temper" published by the Mayo Clinic stipulates, "Instead of focusing on what made you mad, work on resolving the issue at hand. Does your child's messy room drive you crazy? Close the door. Is your partner late for dinner every night? Schedule meals later in the evening — or agree to eat on your own a few times a week. Remind yourself that anger won't fix anything and might only make it worse."

The APA suggests using the energy triggered by anger towards problem solving. "Sometimes, our anger and frustration are caused by very real and inescapable problems in our lives. Not all anger is misplaced, and often it's a healthy, natural response to these difficulties. There is also a cultural belief that every problem has a solution, and it adds to our frustration to find out that this isn't always the case. The best attitude to bring to such a situation, then, is not to focus on finding the solution, but rather on how you handle and face the problem. Make a plan, and check your progress along the way. Resolve to give it your best, but also not to punish yourself if an answer doesn't come right away. If you can approach it with your best intentions and efforts and make a serious attempt to face it head-on, you will be less likely to lose patience and fall into all-or-nothing thinking, even if the problem does not get solved right away."

Humour can release the tension. When things get a bit tense, you can make use of some humour, even self-deprecation, to ease up the tension and diffuse the situation. According to the Mayo Clinic, "lightening up can help diffuse tension. Use humour to help you face what's making you angry and, possibly, any unrealistic expectations you have for how things should go. Avoid sarcasm, though — it can hurt feelings and make things worse."

Some people have the natural gift of saying just the right joke or light-hearted comment when a discussion gets heated or right before tempers flare. Humour can momentarily distract people's attention and even make people forget what it was they were extremely angry about in the first place, even for just a few moments. This momentary break can be enough for you to regain control, and collect yourself before confronting the situation at hand.

Don't hold grudges. People are not perfect. No matter how dear a person is to you, whether he or she is a family member, friend, loved one, colleague, or neighbour, mistakes are bound to happen. People will intentionally or unintentionally cause you pain, heartache, disappointment, regret, or disappointment, in the same way that you will inevitably also cause pain to another person. When someone makes a mistake and apologizes to you or attempts to rectify the situation, forgiving that person not only restores your relationship but also releases you from the burden of holding that grudge for a long time.

Writing for *Psychology Today*, Andrea Brandt, Ph.D. M.F.T. says, "By forgiving, you are accepting the reality of what happened and finding a way to live in a state of resolution with it. This can be a gradual process—and it doesn't necessarily have to include the person you are forgiving. Forgiveness isn't something you do for the person who wronged you; it's something you do for you."

It also helps to put yourself in the other person's shoes, says Dr. Brandt. "He or she is flawed because all human beings are flawed. He or she acted from limited beliefs and a skewed frame of reference because sometimes we all act from our limited beliefs and skewed frames of reference. When you were hurt, the other person was trying to have a need met. What do you think this need was and why did the person go about it in such a hurtful way?"

Forgiveness does not necessarily mean being open to being hurt or taken advantage of again. Rather, it is releasing yourself and deciding to move on, cultivating a mindset of progress. As Dr. Brandt says in her article, "Forgiveness puts the final seal on what happened that hurt you. You will still remember what happened, but you will no longer be bound by it. Having worked through the feelings and learned what you need to do to strengthen your boundaries or get your needs met, you are better able to take care of yourself in the future. Forgiving the other person is a wonderful way to honour yourself. It affirms to the universe that you deserve to be happy."

Improve communication. Many instances that cause anger can be reduced or avoided if communication were to be improved. It is unfair, for instance, to expect people to live up to a certain set of ideals or standards you have not communicated clearly. As an example, if you are planning to meet with colleagues for an important meeting at 9:00 a.m., and need to be out of the meeting by 10:00 a.m. because of another appointment, saying so directly and clearly in your memo or circular to all concerned parties would reiterate to them the need to be there on time, rather than a vague directive to be there "first thing in the morning".

Communication also must be kept clear even in the heat of the moment. The APA says, Angry people tend to jump to—and act on—conclusions, and some of those conclusions can be very inaccurate. The first thing to do if you're in a heated discussion is slow down and think through your responses. Don't say the first thing that comes into your head, but slow down and think carefully about what you want to say. At the same time, listen carefully to what the other person is saying and take your time before answering.

Again, the importance of pausing and reflecting takes center stage. "Listen, too, to what is underlying the anger. For instance, you like a certain amount of freedom and personal space, and your "significant other" wants more connection and closeness. If he or she starts complaining about your activities, don't retaliate by painting your partner as a jailer, a warden, or an albatross around your neck," says the APA. "It's natural to get defensive when you're criticized, but don't fight back. Instead, listen to what's underlying the words: the message that this person might feel neglected and unloved. It may take a lot of patient questioning on your part, and it may require some breathing space, but don't let your anger—or a partner's—let a discussion spin out of control. Keeping your cool can keep the situation from becoming a disastrous one."

Assess your environment. Could it be that you need a change in your environment or immediate circle in order to better control your anger issues and become a calmer person? If you are constantly around people who are negative and engage in bickering or squabbles among themselves, the chances of imbibing this attitude in yourself also greatly increases. On the other hand, you may have a better chance of improving your anger management skills if you are around supportive people who can give you the advice and guidance you need in this effort.

Surround yourself with positive, encouraging, and pleasant people who make you see the good side of life, who give you and other people the benefit of the doubt, and who can honestly and openly discuss maters with you without resorting to blaming, shaming, or negativity. When your environment is full of people who have also seen the importance of controlling anger and keeping frustration in check, you will subconsciously begin to also live this out in your daily life and pick up their best practices.

Take a break. Taking care of yourself regularly is very important in keeping your physical, mental, emotional well-being in check. As already mentioned in a previous chapter, fatigue and exhaustion compound your irritability and make you more prone to angry outbursts. Getting enough rest, and disconnecting yourself from your daily routine from time to time, makes you better able to deal with difficult situations that may be triggers for episodes of anger or frustration.

The APA sites, "Problems and responsibilities can weigh on you and make you feel angry at the "trap" you seem to have fallen into and all the people and things that form that trap. Give yourself a break. Make sure you have some "personal time" scheduled for times of the day that you know are particularly stressful. One example is the working mother who has a standing rule that when she comes home from work, for the first 15 minutes "nobody talks to Mom unless the house is on fire." After this brief quiet time, she feels better prepared to handle demands from her kids without blowing up at them."

Try yoga or meditation. Yoga and meditation techniques have been used by many people all over the world for coping with stress and anger. JC Peter, writing for *Spirituality and Health Magazine,* explains, "Yoga is, in part, a practice for life. It's natural and normal to feel anger, and yoga can help us find the compassionate action that the anger is sometimes trying to point us toward. Disempowering anger is a bitterness that buries itself deep in our guts, disguising the powerlessness, fear, or grief that live in its kernel. This kind of anger is confusing, and its actions are rarely compassionate. Sometimes this bitterness remains after empowering anger has come and gone. You may have done your best to fight injustice, but afterwards injustice still exists.

Peter writes further, "The mindfulness practice of yoga can help us discern what we are feeling: Is this anger empowering or disempowering? It can also physically move excess energy, especially when we stimulate Manipura Chakra, an energy center located in the solar plexus. It's right where you feel anger, fear and anxiety."

Breathing deeply when you are feeling angry also greatly helps in anger management, and breathing exercises are an intrinsic part of yoga. As *LiveStrong.com* says in the article "Yoga Poses for Anger," "You may have heard that when you're angry, you should take a deep breath and count to 10. Yoga has a similar approach. Simply taking a deep breath the moment you feel angry and noticing the way the emotions affect your mind can be a powerful way to diffuse a potentially explosive situation. More precise yoga breath work, such as alternate nostril breathing or Bhastrika, aka Bellow's, breath can also clear your mind to ease anger."

Meditation is also closely related to yoga, and can also help you in better managing your anger levels. Tanya Gold, a writer for the Health and Wellbeing section of *The Guardian,* talks about meditation, "It seems that meditation does have health benefits, particularly for neurotics with anger and anxiety issues such as myself. This week American academics published the results of their research into the joys of transcendental meditation (TM). Apparently guinea pigs (human ones) who practised TM showed a 48% decline in depressive symptoms. Last year another study indicated that there were 47% fewer heart attacks, strokes and premature deaths among transcendental meditation-heads, which tunes in with what my friend Yogi Cameron, the former male supermodel, has told me. 'Yogis,' he once said, 'choose when to die'."

The APA suggests some breathing techniques for managing anger: "Breathe deeply, from your diaphragm; breathing from your chest won't relax you. Picture your breath coming up from your "gut." Slowly repeat a calm word or phrase such as "relax," "take it easy." Repeat it to yourself while breathing deeply. Use imagery; visualize a relaxing experience, from either your memory or your imagination. Nonstrenuous, slow yoga-like exercises can relax your muscles and make you feel much calmer. Practice these techniques daily. Learn to use them automatically when you're in a tense situation."

Seek help if needed. If your anger issues have gotten out of control, and more so if your anger management efforts are being hindered by underlying medical conditions or mental health problems, seek professional help for managing your anger. The earlier you can get expert assistance; the more problems you can avoid later on. Do not wait for your anger issues to become so compounded that they begin to have a disastrous effect on your relationships, family ties, friendships, work performance, and other connections. Help can be obtained, and you can win over any anger issues you are facing.

According to the APA, a therapist or mental health professional can assess where you are and figure out the best possible way to handle your anger. "If you feel that your anger is really out of control, if it is having an impact on your relationships and on important parts of your life, you might consider counselling to learn how to handle it better. A psychologist or other licensed mental health professional can work with you in developing a range of techniques for changing your thinking and your behaviour. When you talk to a prospective therapist, tell her or him that you have problems with anger that you want to work on, and ask about his or her approach to anger management. Make sure this isn't only a course of action designed to "put you in touch with your feelings and express them"—that may be precisely what your problem is. With counselling, psychologists say, a highly angry person can move closer to a middle range of anger in about 8 to 10 weeks, depending on the circumstances and the techniques used."

Conclusion

Anger, as with any other human emotion, must be harnessed and managed properly as an essential aspect of life. As you seek to manage your anger issues, your motivation should be to come out of it a better, more balanced person who is better equipped to handle different situations and keep your temper in control even under pressure. The ultimate goal is self-development, although you will also notice that as you have a better handle on your temper and irritability, the quality of your relationships with those in your inner circle as well as your sphere of influence will greatly improve.

Anger management is an ongoing process that should start somewhere but should not cease. As you get in touch with what causes you to become angry, and figure out ways to deal with these stimuli, the focus of anger management should shift from one common situation or trigger to another until you have sorted out the various causes and come up with rational ways of dealing with each one.

While anger cannot be completely eliminated, your reactions to it can certainly be improved. The APA asserts, "Remember, you can't eliminate anger—and it wouldn't be a good idea if you could. In spite of all your efforts, things will happen that will cause you anger; and sometimes it will be justifiable anger. Life will be filled with frustration, pain, loss, and the unpredictable actions of others. You can't change that; but you can change the way you let such events affect you. Controlling your angry responses can keep them from making you even more unhappy in the long run."

www.ingramcontent.com/pod-product-compliance
Lightning Source LLC
Chambersburg PA
CBHW061939280526
45787CB00004B/1653